A Catafalque
For Ann

First published 2021

Copyright © Colin Stern 2021

The right of Colin Stern to be identified as the author of this work has been asserted in accordance with the Copyright, Designs & Patents Act 1988.

All rights reserved. No part of this book may be reproduced, stored in a retrieval system, or transmitted in any form or by any means, electronic, electrostatic, magnetic tape, mechanical, photocopying, recording or otherwise, without the written permission of the copyright holder.

Published under licence by Brown Dog Books and The Self-Publishing Partnership Ltd, 10b Greenway Farm, Bath Rd, Wick, nr. Bath BS30 5RL

www.selfpublishingpartnership.co.uk

ISBN printed book: 978-1-83952-341-0

ISBN e-book: 978-1-83952-342-7

Cover design by Kevin Rylands

Internal design by Andrew Easton

Printed and bound in the UK

This book is printed on FSC certified paper

A Catafalque For Ann

Colin Stern

Dedication

My Ann passed on a year ago
And left me with my love.
She needed a remembrance, though
She's buried by a grove.
I wrote these verses as I grieved
And marked the passing times.
So let her friends these words receive,
My dedication rhymes.

For Ann

The secretary's useful
She wrote a pretty hand
And, as I must be truthful,
Was not a one-night stand.

She came to work one morning
And quickly caught my eye.
Her beauty had me fawning
I cannot tell a lie.

We went out for a pizza
And to the cinema.
Her name was Ann, not Lisa.
She liked my sporty car.

We spent a year together
And then agreed to part.
That day was stormy weather
And lightning struck my heart.

She emigrated, crossing
The wide Atlantic sea.
Her vessel took a tossing
But made the distant quay.

She lived there for a season
I tried to keep in touch.
My love the only reason,
I needed her too much.

We took a short vacation
And then she came back home.
The cause of my elation
When at the aerodrome.

She said we could be married
I walked her down the aisle.
Our lives have been so varied,
But always with a smile.

But she's no longer living.
Death took her in his arms
Her ending unforgiving,
No recollection calms.

A year ago her passing
And still I weep. Unfair.
Mortality trespassing
Upon my lonely care.

When First We Met

When first we met
We shared a pizza meal.
I shan't forget.

I paid the debt,
Succumbed to your appeal,
When first we met.

I couldn't get
A sense that you were real,
When first we met.

My course is set.
Affection all I feel,
When first we met.

An easy bet
My heart would never heal
When first we met.

I love you yet.
I heard your death knell peal.
I shan't forget
When first we met.

PRELUDE

Remembering your life before you fell
Into dementia's slowly creeping claws
You lived it to the full and loved it well
With friends and family without a pause.

Your golf was skilful, played with striking poise.
Together we won trophies, made our mark.
You shopped for golf clothes, clubs and other toys
Sparkled with fun before your world went dark.

Your eyes betrayed you, took away your car.
You blamed me for it; freedom torn away.
Though treatment helped, it could not break the bar
To all your pleasures, taken from the day.

At the beginning, odd behaviour came
Seen by our children, puzzled at the sight.
Some time until we knew what was to blame
And cursed the fate that gave you such a blight.

I had an inkling of the likely cause,
But had to wait until you ready were
To seek a diagnosis, open doors
That might be better closed, no more demur.

DEMENTIA

We visited the clinic, you and I,
Seeking to find the reason you forget.
You tried to answer questions. By and by
Criteria for dementia had been met.

Alzheimer, this disease they said at first,
Though I was doubtful that they'd got it right.
Your odd behaviour made me fear the worst
And in Australia they brought the light.

Degeneration of your brain, it's true,
But frontotemporal in type, they thought.
Untreatable of course, so there were few
Years left for you, and yet how hard you fought.

And slowly, bit by bit, it chipped away
At what you are, and were, and then were not.
But, underneath it all, your soul did stay,
And what we had could never be forgot.

You lost your limbs, became dependent on
My nursing, less than perfect though it was.
As carers came and went, all sense was gone
Of dignity. Routines became our cause.

So, as you neared your end, I sat with you,
Through hours of anguish at your suffering.
Until you breathed your last. Our final view
Together, sorrow lets no buffering.

As months have passed, my grief matures in pain,
And little things remind me of our life.
Our closeness as you died was not in vain,
We have become the perfect man and wife.

Death

I nursed you in your final hours,
Dazed.
To save you was beyond my powers.
Phased.
I rinsed your mouth and wiped your brow,
Amazed
At how you fought to live somehow.
Blazed
With anger that you had to leave.
Raised
Your head to mine, a touch receive,
Gazed
Upon your face a final time.
Eased
Your passing from these arms of mine,
Deceased.

Gone

While you were here you filled my every hour;
We struggled hard together to stay whole.
But saving you was not within my power
And losing you has ripped apart my soul.
Dementia's march is patently unfair
Creeping so slowly 'til at last you're gone.
Recovery requires me to repair
To find within me purpose to go on.
I shall be haunted by your watching ghost
Seeing you in the corner of my eye.
Within my silence, I'll be hearing most,
Those soft exchanges made 'twixt you and I.
Departure, though expected was a shock.
Death came like thunder, shattering my rock.

Funerary Tribute

She stood beside us as we learned of life,
Holding our hands to guide our falt'ring feet.
Acting our strongest shield when risk was rife.
Whatever danger threatened, she would meet.
Always encouraging, never hind'ring us,
Hoping our hopes and stretching out our reach.
Letting us lead our lives without a fuss:
Charlotte and Jonathan, lending strength to each.
Seeing us grown, she forged another place,
Playing at tennis 'n' golf with equal zest.
Flashing her smile, she made new friends with grace,
Stolen away as illness took her best.
Ann left too early, toppled from her peak,
Yet, through her children, let her nature speak.

Ann

I miss you.
Despite anticipation, when
Death comes, its shock is vast
And overwhelming. Sudden then
My thoughts about our past.
I miss you.

I miss you.
There are few ways to show my grief
That measure up to loss.
I cannot weep or wail, I'd lief
Pull mourning veils across.
I miss you.

I miss you.
There's little point to life from now,
Save struggling to the end.
A single furrow must I plough,
A lonely road to wend.
I miss you.

I miss you.
I think about your love of life,
But can't forget your death.
I'm haunted by my living wife,
I feel her scented breath.
I miss you.

I miss you.
I cared for you in those last years,
When much of you had fled.
You never shed deservéd tears
Your suffering had bred.
I miss you.

I miss you.
I think about light-hearted times,
When children ran about
And we read tales and nursery rhymes
And laughed at all and nowt.
I miss you.

I miss you.
But know that I must try
To lift my spirits up.
To raise my aspirations high
And fill my empty cup.
I miss you.

I miss you.
So, at my death, when my times end,
I join you underground.
I'll look at you and we will mend,
Our love again be found.
I missed you.

The Hole

There's a vast, gaping hole in my life;
It's the loss of my lovely late wife.
Still present throughout this bleak house,
A tangible, frangible spouse.

She appears when I least expect,
A spectre that I can't direct.
Small fragments remind me of her,
Act as a fresh memory spur.

Mementos stop me in my tracks,
Reminding me what my life lacks.
I forget what I wanted to do,
Thinking only of what we went through.

I try not to think of the years
When you suffered your illness. My fears
That your passing would not bring us peace
Have come true, there is no surcease.

I'm hoping in time I'll adjust.
Finding solace is something I must
Try to find, if my life's to progress
And reduce my emotional stress.

Despair

My empty heart is aching for relief.
Its chambers echo with my lonely feet,
Whose dragging paces signify defeat,
Monotonous percussion of my grief.
The sound of silence permeates my soul
The voices heard are everywhere but here.
When people call, their sympathy's sincere
Though nothing helps regenerate my whole.
This isn't living, only going on.
Lacking in purpose, day follows empty day.
Journeying into fog until I fall,
Careless of danger, all I value gone.
There's no direction, nothing lights the way
To a kind harbour. I've no hope at all.

AGNOSTICISM

I don't believe in afterlife.
Religion has its place,
But can't revive my sleeping wife
Nor shape her smiling face.

A faith's a comfort, people say,
And need its warming glow.
They pray to God each mournful day
And hope that hope will grow.

Religion's only lying, just
A false way laid ahead.
Our life is all and so we must
Accept our final bed.

To make a fiction of us both,
Joined in some future place,
As though we'd once more plight our troth:
I know it's not the case.

So I must try to live and love
And keep your flame alight.
I feel your presence with me move
And make my living bright.

You won't be there to say goodbye
When time to pop my clogs.
Perhaps, in death, we'll kiss and cry
In cloying mists and fogs.

The Visit

I placed a yellow rose upon your grave
Plucked from our garden, still in perfect shape.
It lay, as symbol of the love you gave
Until you died. From grief there's no escape.

This pilgrimage, my first trip to the place
Where now you lie, in willow coffin laid.
A green slate stone embedded, on its face
Inscription so your mem'ry doesn't fade.

I stood and thought about the life we had,
Remembering our sorrows and our joy.
But mostly joy that made our living glad
And full of sunlight, happy girl and boy.

Our children have their children to console
And keep them focused on what lies ahead.
My memories must keep your spirit whole.
I mourn you often, as I lie abed.

I shall revisit you in months to come
Standing and wishing that you still were here.
But, for the moment, while my heart is numb,
I face a future that seems dark and drear.

Your Photograph

Your photograph looks blandly back at me
Watching at supper, breakfast, lunch and tea.
A passport photo, blown a little up,
Eyed from the rim of each refreshing cup.

Six other pictures line the windowsill.
In each you smile or laugh, are carefree still.
But your unsmiling image is more real,
And I can talk to you; more natural feel.

Is it unhealthy to keep loving you?
To cultivate your memory, revive a few
Of many happy days when all was well
And you were free of harsh dementia's spell?

I do not think so. I keep watching out
To stay within this life. To look about
I focus on the living while I'm here
Because they need me: death can hold no fear.

Grandchildren sparkle, they immortal feel.
'You'll be a hundred, you've a healthy deal'
They tell me. They're too young to understand
Your passing changed security to sand.

No matter. My remaining half must do
What we did as a whole: one half was you.
I'll not permit your memory to fade,
Nor let you slide away into the shade.

Staying Alive

I use routine to keep me sane
My life is ordered thus.
I find that structure, in the main
Makes living less a fuss.

Since Annie passed away, I cling
To each familiar task.
The daily work I do does bring
The comfort that I ask.

I rise each morning, break my fast
And either golf or run.
And, once my exercise is past
Have coffee and a bun.

And then I write: a children's book
Or poetry. Instead
Another job, I iron, or cook
Or rest upon my bed.

I'm rarely idle, every hour
I plan something to do.
But dwell on mem'ries sweet, none sour,
That marked my life with you.

The actions give a purpose to
The road that lies ahead.
Without them, I'd be wading through
A lake of molten lead.

'What is my life,' I contemplate
'Without my other half?'
To reconcile my severed state
I need a stronger staff.

Time is your healer, I am told
I don't believe it's true.
I will not let my love grow cold,
I'm not forgetting you.

No Therapy

The bullrush beds beside this quiet lake
Hide duckling, moorhen, even heron pairs.
Soft breezes sway them in the gentle airs
Though nothing here does consolation make.
The azure sky has cotton wool for clouds,
Fantastic shapes that childhood helped us see
No longer hold such interest for me,
Preferring solitude, away from crowds.
Unhealthy meditation I indulge
To contemplate the loss of all I loved.
My perfect life destroyed by what has proved,
To fit the sad prognoses they divulge.
Warm Southern winds can't carry off my cares,
Nor nature wash away my dark despairs.

Solitary

I walk along the towpath on my own,
A journey that I've made in sweeter times.
The wind is bitter; chilling to the bone,
And swirls the leaves descending from the limes.

The river carries ripples of regret,
Watching me pass alone this autumn day.
Behind those woods the orange sun will set,
Taking both light and happiness away.

I know I'm in the twilight of my life
And isolation worries at my soul.
It adds to feelings of my loss of wife.
I hope to heal, as I'm no longer whole.

The crunching leaf noise punctuates my walk,
Alleviating silence in their death.
A passing couple chatters, and their talk
Displays their misty tracery of breath.

The riverbank in summer is alive,
With families and children on their bikes.
They buzz like bees about a busy hive
An atmosphere that everybody likes.

I hope next summer I'll be happy too,
Although I find it hard to think of that.
My long depression must not injure you,
I'll try to offer you more cheerful chat.

Without You

Living alone, our debris lies
Around me. It maintains our ties.
I try to keep my life intact.
It feels to me like entr'acte.

I'm balancing 'twixt us and death,
Knowing it's closer with each breath.
My days are filled with minor things
Uncertain what each morning brings.

I try to find some pleasure still.
It takes some forcing of my will.
I search for purposes, but fail
To find a way, a path, a trail.

I punctuate each little task
With thoughts of you and what you'd ask.
I know you know I'm killing time
Until I'm lying under lime.

As I grow older, I will change
My features slowly rearrange.
So, when we meet again, you'll see
Some alterations, though it's me.

And, in the future, when life ends
My lasting life must make amends
For all those good times that you missed
And moments when you were not kissed.

Recollections

The house I live in has an empty feel
It's full of spaces where you used to be.
A ghostly presence that seems all too real
Which catches at my soul, won't set me free.

I enter rooms in which you used to sit
And see you in the corner of my eye.
Your armchair, occupied and dimly lit,
Invades my consciousness, evokes a sigh.

You drop suggestions in my silent ear
Urging me on, to find epiphany.
Moments of laughter, painful sounds to hear,
Past conversations echoing in me.

Some widows banish images from view
Hoping by doing so to limit grief.
I won't erase my haunted thoughts of you
I'm not in search of memory relief.

I'm glad that you're still here. I hope you'll stay.
Together we formed everything in life.
Although the future may be dull and grey,
It's lit by recollections of my wife.

Christmas With(out) Ann

Our children think I'm Christmassing alone
Now that you've fled beyond my stretching arms.
They worry that I'll sit, chew on a bone,
So send me messages with false alarms.

But they don't understand that you're still here,
Sitting and listening to my feeble jokes.
Smiling a little, saying 'Yes, my dear,'
At humour that would piss off other folks.

I'm making sure that Christmas lunch is good,
With pheasant, not a turkey, for a change.
I'll cook for both of us. Outstanding food
Presented well, the best I can arrange.

An English sparkling rosé to begin,
With quail eggs and smoked salmon on the side.
And, with the bird, roast tatties, sprouts, a sin
Not to include the lot, just 'cos you died.

I cannot toast your health, but memory
Is best; those special times we filled with love.
Your presence may be extra sensory,
But that's enough to fit me like a glove.

And, when the meal is over we shall sit,
Have conversation without needing words.
Feeling at ease, when soothing lamps are lit,
Knowing that we have feasted as do lords.

There's nothing maudlin in this dreaming on,
But healthy understanding of my loss.
Although your living body may have gone,
Your essence still to me will come across.

New Year

The year you died has flown away,
Its days have dusty ended.
Your dying day was cold and grey,
And my heart's not yet mended.

The sudden rift was nature's gift,
A cruel cut to lovers.
I've only memories to sift
That fleeting thought uncovers.

I sit with you, a friendly ghost,
And toast New Year's beginning.
A time you ever loved the most,
Your smile at its most winning.

The grandchildren may want your hug
Our children lack your kisses.
They need far less my ugly mug,
It's you that each one misses.

I mustn't mope; they care for me,
They call and ask and check,
Say 'Are you well?' but cannot see
I'm not, but what the heck!

I see the next year stretch in front,
But know not where I'm heading
Though wit's still sharp, emotion's blunt
And tears I'm still a'shedding.

I know I'll never be the same,
You moulded me forever
No other one could stake a claim
Or heal that awful sever.

Purposelessness

There's little purpose in my empty life
Moving from hollow day to vacant night.
Losing my partner Ann, my lovely wife
Makes my existence seem a pointless fight.

Planning activities to fill the time
Endlessly stretching out in front of me
Doesn't fit reason, let alone make rhyme.
There is no point to it that I can see.

Lying in bed at night, the silence wraps
Around me, is appropriately blank.
I try to find the ways to fill the gaps
In living. It seems futile, to be frank.

Covid's a hindrance, locking me inside.
Out for nine holes of golf, when it is fine,
My only social contact since you died.
Wait for my vaccination, in the line.

How will I manage, once I am set free?
Is there a point in going on like this?
I need objectives, do you not agree?
It's being useful; that is what I miss.

Birthday 2021

This birthday is the first one since you passed,
The first time that we shall not celebrate
Together. Time without you goes so fast
The days between us grow at pace; don't wait.

Seven and seventy candles should have been
The number on your cake. They did not come.
This year of grief continues. We've not seen
Our much loved lover: granny, wife and mum.

Your empty chair seems emptier today,
An anniversary without a guest
Of honour. When your spirit went away
What left was everything I valued best.

But still I'll raise my glass and drink to you
Not health, but memory will be the toast.
Your photographs are in my constant view,
Allowing me to act here as your host.

Will there be many more days such as these?
Who knows, but while I'm here they'll carry on.
I'll keep your flame alive and so appease
The rack your absence places me upon.

Healing Conversation

I saw a friend who'd lost his wife, like me.
We met by chance and, seeing I was free,
I asked him in for coffee and a chat.
We sat there for a little, chewed the fat.

Eventually our conversation moved,
Discussing how we'd lost the ones we'd loved.
A painful subject, easier to bear
With someone with an understanding ear.

It's typical, each day, that we rehearse
The way it happened, how we learned to nurse.
Small things remind us of those awful times
That led up the tolling of death's chimes.

When you're alone, these flashbacks hit you hard,
Events that cut you deep and left you scarred.
Though different, we found it much the same;
The odd way that we both accepted blame.

Although you know you're in no way at fault,
Into our wounds these feelings added salt.
But sharing such experience with him
Made memories like these a touch less grim.

We parted and he cycled to the gate,
Having adjusted better to our fate.
Somehow we knew this chat would help us heal,
Nudging our move to a more even keel.

Shared Pain

Thank you for telling me about your life
Your family adventures and your spouse,
Your love for him and your delightful house,
Where you performed the duties of a wife.
Thank you for inviting me to share
The pain you suffered at your husband's death
And how you listened to his dying breath,
That tore your soul apart and laid you bare.
We've both experienced that searing loss,
The wound that never seems to heal at all,
Though distance helps to dull the ache a bit.
We suffer nights in which we pitch and toss,
The utter darkness an enclosing wall.
We hope eventually a scar will knit.

Transitions

Once we were two and then we were one,
Now I'm alone and it isn't much fun.
Trying to cope now I'm only a half,
I struggle on with nary a laugh.

Thinking of you makes me feel blue,
What we had then, what we went through.
Those left behind strengthen my mind.
No kin more kind could anyone find.

Making up plans gives my life shape,
Though from my sadness there's no escape.
Structure is good at keeping me straight,
Got to keep going, 'cos life doesn't wait.

Where should I go, what lies ahead?
I mustn't mope or keep to my bed.
Poetry helps to show me the way,
Searching for sun when everything's grey.

Talking with friends who suffered the same
Makes me feel useful, helping the lame.
They understand just what it is like
Robbed of a partner, grief's grievous strike.

Will there be sunlight over the hill?
Are there yet promises I can fulfil?
No one can know the future, I know
Hope is the tonic from which it will flow.

What's Love?

What ancient instinct made us choose to be
Together on life's journey, as a pair?
A hormone that stole softly through the air?
An impulse that united you and me?
Perhaps it's preordained, with no escape.
Inevitable consequence alone,
Genetic limitation, in the bone,
Not chosen by us, but genetic rape.
It mattered little, once we fell in love,
Though how that happened, I have not a clue;
It seemed so seamless in its harmony.
A symbiosis in a single move
That made one person out of me and you.
Now that you're gone, I'm left with half of me.

In Memoriam

Ten months have passed since last we kissed
Those days you've been unseen;
The hours together that we've missed,
The times that might have been.

I lie in solitary state
And think death was unfair
To come so soon and not to wait
'Til we could part a pair.

Your leaving left a searing wound
That slowly forms a scar.
An injury that's so profound
It changes who we are.

As time has passed I better see
The perfect life we had.
Our tragedy has moulded me,
Extracting good from bad.

I'll bring our friends to celebrate
The partnership we made.
A party held so we can fête
You, with your life displayed.

With glasses raised to drink to you
To memories so sweet.
And though your face has gone from view,
Imagine that we meet.

Dislocation

Sitting and staring at confining walls
You realise new friendships must be made.
Without another, conversation falls
Into the empty spaces, words will fade.

Man is a social animal, requires
Interdependence for his better health.
Such contacts serve to satisfy desires,
Enrich one's being, one's internal wealth.

You join new friendly groups, perhaps to walk,
And drift between the others, much the same
As you. They all are desperate to talk
Of work and life and loss and who's to blame.

One woman seeks you out each time you go;
Seems keen to tell you all her private life.
You don't avoid her, but you let her know,
So gently, you're not looking for a wife.

Another man has suffered, much like you.
You often walk together, sharing thought.
It's comforting to hear another's view
And sympathise with him, and so you ought.

You start to comprehend how much you lost
When your life partner left your partnership.
You can't recover this enormous cost,
But seek some solace in fresh fellowship.

There can be life beyond your fading grief,
Although it takes its time to manifest.
You mingle, searching out for new relief,
But often feeling an unwelcome guest.

Thoughts on a Friend's Death

Words can't express the sadness that I feel

When friends pass on and we are left behind.

My welling tears conspire to make me blind,

While following life's unforgiving wheel.

My turn will come, my family will cry

As round my grave they gather in lament.

They'll ruminate on how my time was spent

Then leave me underground, the earth my sky,

Next to my precious Ann. We'll join in death,

The years between will pass as fast as light

The grass will grow and sad trees wave their leaves

As breezes ruffle them with gentle breath.

We had our time and though we're out of sight,

Long dead, we'll know our family still grieves.

Elegy

When leaves last grew upon that tree,
Your life had almost passed.
I sat and watched, you looked at me
And softly breathed your last.

The season's cycles circle on,
Inevitable, slow.
It's now a year since you've been gone
And still it hurts me so.

The steady ticking of the clock
Acknowledges my life.
I sit and listen, taking stock
Of my beloved wife.

My pain is constant, aches and throbs
With negativity.
There's no relief from evening sobs
That emanate from me.

My zest for life has fled away,
I'm one-dimensional.
The future's looking less than gay
Without my only gal.

A Catafalque for Ann